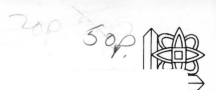

Herbs in Pots

SEARCH PRESS

Introduction

Growing herbs in pots is a splendid occupation for lazy gardeners, or those with a small garden or none at all. Many fresh herbs are never available in shops and packets of dry herbs are no substitute; the alternative is to grow your own.

When I started growing herbs, I read many books about it. I was utterly confused by the different opinions on how, what and where: so many composts containing this, that and the other; and so on. I decided to use a seed compost for the seeds and a potting compost for the plants. I mixed the two if I was short of one.

Basic guidelines follow for growing all the herbs in this book. Specific notes are given on each page.

Cultivation

You can buy herb seed packets from most nurserymen, and there are specialist suppliers in most countries; their addresses can be obtained from directories.

Seed trays are unnecessary as you will probably want at the most six pots of each herb. Disposable plastic coffee cups are ideal for seeds. You can also use yoghurt cartons. Wash the cups and cut a drainage hole in the bottom of each one. Using a good seed compost (it should be moist), fill to within 1.5cm (½") of the top. Put four seeds, slightly apart, in each cup and sprinkle with a little more compost. Arrange the cups on a tray or piece of hardboard and slide this into a large plastic bag. Carefully transfer everything to a dark place under the bed, for instance.

Inspect the cups each morning and evening. As soon as the seedlings appear remove the cups from the bag and place them on a windowsill facing south, east or west.

Transplant seedlings to a larger pot when the first two seed-leaves are fully formed, but before the true leaves appear. Choose the healthiest seedlings (not those with very long straggly stems). Fill the bottom of the plant pot with a few pebbles and a little sand (if you can get hold of it). Use a good brand of potting compost (your supplier will advise you). The compost should be moist, never bone-dry or soaking wet.

General care

Most herbs originate in warm climates and are used to infrequent rainfall. Never over-water your plants as that will rot the roots. When the compost feels dry round the edge of the pot, water the plant. Use rain water; if you haven't any use tepid water.

Herbs are best just before the plant flowers. Pick your leaves from the top and remove any which are yellow.

Allow your herbs some fresh air occasionally (but never put them in a direct draught) and spray them at intervals with tepid water — you can buy small hand sprays from nurserymen and garden centres.

You will enjoy growing herbs and cooking with them. It is fascinating to watch an aromatic herb develop from a tiny seed.

SEEDS

SEED COMPOST

LOTS OF
COFFEE CUPS
OR
YOGHURT
CARTONS

LABELS TO
IDENTIFY SEEDS

AN OLD
TABLESPOON
IS USEFUL

PEBBLES FOR
DRAINAGE

SEED COMPOST

HAND
SPRAY

POTTING COMPOST

VARIOUS
PLANT POTS

POTTING COMPOST

Horehound

Horehound is a hardy perennial which reaches a height of 60cm (24"). It can be found growing wild in wasteland areas of Britain. The leaves are grey-green, oval and serrated; they are furry to the touch and deeply veined. The square stems have a soft down and, where the leaves join, produce small clusters of tiny white flowers which bloom in midsummer. Because of the interesting texture of leaves and stems, horehound is frequently used for flower arrangements.

cultivation

Read notes on cultivation (page 2). The seeds should germinate within a week to ten days. Once you have transplanted the seedlings put them where the sun shines for at least part of the day. Horehound prefers a dryish soil so do not over-water. Cut a little off the top stems to encourage bushy growth.

culinary

Horehound leaves are rather bitter and strongly aromatic when eaten raw, but an infusion can be made more palatable by the addition of clear honey and fresh lemon juice. The unsweetened infusion is sometimes used as a skin lotion for eczema. Horehound is an attractive plant but is now mainly grown for its ancient historical associations. It is one of the oldest medicinal herbs recorded.

medicinal

Horehound has a reputation among herbalists as an excellent remedy for coughs, colds, bronchitis, sore throats and asthma. It is also considered to have a calming effect on bad nerves and tension; but do not over-indulge — the tea is mildly laxative.

historical

Horehound is also called white horehound. Some say that the name comes from an old English word meaning greyish white: others that the Greeks used the plant as an antidote for mad dog bites — hence its name. But herbalists from 800 AD to the present day agree on the benefits of the herb.

Sage

Sage is a hardy shrub-like perennial. Its cultivation is a peasant industry in some parts of northern Europe. It grows wild in dry parts of the USA and it is a popular pot herb in Britain. It grows to approximately 60cm (24"). Its large oval grey-green leaves release a pungent aroma when rubbed between thumb and finger. The small flowers are usually lilac but sometimes pale blue and bloom from May to July.

cultivation

Read the general notes on cultivation (page 2). Many people find that sage is slow to grow and that leaves cannot be harvested until at least a year after sowing. The plant opposite was sown in the March and photographed in the August of the same year. Although sage is a perennial it has to be replaced after about four years.

culinary

As almost everyone knows sage and onion make an excellent stuffing for rich poultry and meats. Sage can also be used in liver, goose or duck patés, meat loaves and sausages — but don't use too much or the strong sage flavour will overpower everything else. It can be added to fish soups and goes well in dishes whose main ingredient is cheddar cheese. Sage jelly is an interesting dessert and is sometimes eaten with fresh fruit salad and home-made ice cream.

medicinal

Like the previous herb, sage aids digestion, and so it is used with rich meats. As a tea (using fresh or dried leaves), it is recommended for coughs, colds, headaches and feverishness. As a mouth wash, it is said to relieve mouth ulcers and sore gums.

historical

The Greeks and Romans used to rub snake bites and sores with sage leaves and even today some people use a sage infusion to treat skin ailments. The Chinese were very fond of sage tea and for many years it was preferred to ordinary tea. In late Victorian times sage was recommended as a dandruff cure.

Lemon Balm

Lemon balm (Melissa balm) is a hardy perennial. It is a native of the Mediterranean but is often found in southern England or Ireland. The plant can grow to a height of 60cm (24″) and its leaves are heart-shaped, serrated and well-veined. Its small cream flowers bloom from July to September.

cultivation

Read general notes on cultivation (page 2). I have often given the seeds up for lost, used the compost for other seeds and then discovered little balms springing up among the thyme and basil. Be patient. See that the compost in the cups hasn't become dry. If it has, stand the cups in a dish of water until the compost feels moist.

culinary

As the name suggests, balm has a delicate lemon flavour. It can be used generously without any risk of overpowering most dishes. Add a handful of washed and finely chopped leaves to white sauce for chicken, ham, fish and lamb. It can be used in all salads or added to cottage cheese and plain yoghurt. It adds a slight lemon tang to puddings and desserts — crab apple jelly, apple pies and tarts, custards and fresh fruit salads.

medicinal

A tea made from balm leaves is said to promote relaxation and to ease restless sleep, and to be a mild remedy for upset tummies and biliousness and to be suitable for most children over long periods. Some say that balm leaves eaten raw will promote sweating and relieve feverish colds and flu.

historical

The Romans brought balm to Britain from the Mediterranean, although it came originally from the Middle East. The botanical name, *Melissa offinalis*, comes from the Greek word for honey bee. The Greeks planted balm round their bee hives believing that it would encourage the bees to stay.

9

Thyme

Thyme is a hardy perennial which grows freely in many parts of the world including Britain. The tiny leaves are evergreen, grow in pairs and are grey-green in colour. The stems change from green to purple and then to wood. The main stems appear to creep along the ground while new growth stretches upwards. Small mauve flowers bloom from May to July. The whole plant is heavily scented. It can grow to a height of 20cm (8") and frequently the width is double the height.

cultivation

Read notes on cultivation (page 2). The seeds should germinate within a week of sowing. The established plant will drink rather more than most other herbs, but don't over-water it or it will become water-logged and the roots will rot. Thyme is a sun-lover and is best placed on a south-facing windowsill.

culinary

Thyme is a strong-flavoured aromatic herb and should be used sparingly. Thin slices of ox liver are very tasty when coated with seasoned flour and a level tablespoon of fresh thyme leaves; serve with buttered mashed potatoes and green beans. Thyme can be used in patés and sausages and makes a pleasant change when added to boiled long-grain rice. It goes well with parsley to make a white sauce for haddock and cod.

medicinal

The oil from thyme has antiseptic qualities and was once an ingredient of disinfectants. Only one teaspoonful of fresh leaves makes a pint of a tea which some say can relieve asthmatic conditions, catarrhal bronchitis and sinus troubles. Taken with honey it is said to soothe sore throats.

historical

Thyme was an ingredient of the incense cones which the Greeks used in their temples. Later, it was added to other herbs and made into a small posy carried by judges and other dignitaries in the belief that it would protect the carriers from the odours and diseases of the poor.

Nasturtium

Nasturtium is a hardy annual and a well-known garden plant. There are two varieties — the dwarf which becomes quite bushy and is used for borders and window boxes, and the climber which sends off trailers and is used to cover walls, banks, and so on. Nasturtium is also grown among vegetables because many pests dislike the essence secreted from its roots. The flowers bloom from June to October and are brilliant red, yellow and orange.

cultivation

Read the notes on cultivation (page 2). Seeds should germinate within a week of sowing. They are about the size of a dried pea, so allow only two to each coffee cup. Four or five seedlings may be transplanted into a large plant pot. The flowering season can be prolonged by removing faded blooms.

culinary

All parts of this plant — leaves, petals and seeds have culinary uses. The leaves have a strong but not unpleasant peppery flavour. Baked in alternate layers with mushrooms and covered with a garlic dressing they make a tasty supper dish. They also make nutritious sandwiches between slices of whole-wheat bread and butter. The fresh flower petals are an attractive addition to green salads and the seeds can be used as a substitute for capers.

medicinal

The high vitamin C content of nasturtium leaves makes the plant a valuable addition to a collection of herbs. The leaves and flowers are claimed to have blood-purifying qualities, and it has been said that a hot poultice made with the crushed seeds can have a beneficial effect on skin ulcers.

historical

Nasturtiums are thought to have come from South America but the idea of using the petals in salads came from the East. In his *English Herbal* John Gerard says that he first received nasturtium seeds from France in 1597. Later, the leaves were used in attempts to improve defective sight.

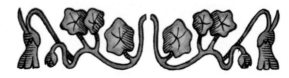

Bay

The bay is a shrub-like tree which can grow to a height of 4m (12') or more. It originates in the Mediterranean region but survives as a garden tree in southern England and is more often grown in tubs and large pots. Bay leaves are elliptical and taper to a point. They are dark green on the upper side, yellowy-green underneath and feel leathery to the touch. Mature trees have small, pale green flowers which bloom in May. These are followed by purple, single-seeded berries.

cultivation

It is possible to grow a bay tree from seed but germination does not always occur. It might save wasted effort if a small plant is bought from a local nursery. The bay prefers some shade in the summer and will survive most conditions, except frost, so bring it indoors during winter. Wipe the leaves occasionally with a damp cloth.

culinary

The bay is used as a spicing agent and only one or two leaves are generally needed. Its flavour is strengthened after slow drying in a dark place. The leaves can be added to braised beef, rabbit stew, vegetable soups, casseroles, goulash and poultry stuffing. I always include one in curries. Bacon pancakes are 'spiced up' by the addition of half a crushed leaf; remember to add one when marinating fish or meat.

medicinal

Bay leaves are known to stimulate the appetite. A tea may be made from three leaves to a pint of boiling water. Nicholas Culpeper, the seventeenth-century English apothecary, recommended the tea as a pain reliever and a remedy for ear and skin troubles. The tea is also supposed to alleviate indigestion.

historical

The Greeks made crowns from bay leaves to honour heroes and poets. The botanical name for bay is *Lauris nobilis,* hence the title 'Poet Laureate'. For centuries branches of bay were strewn on floors because of their scent and alleged antiseptic qualities. They were also kept to ward off evil.

Mint

All varieties of mint are hardy perennials. Those opposite are spearmint, apple (or Bowles) mint and eau de Cologne. Spearmint grows to about 45cm (18"), has an upright stem and narrow dark-green leaves which are finely serrated. Apple mint grows from 60 to 120cm (2' – 4') and has round, slightly woolly leaves. Eau de Cologne has wandering stems and round smooth green leaves with a tinge of purple. All these mints have mauvish spiked flowers which bloom from July to September.

cultivation

It is very difficult to grow mint from seed. Small plants can be bought from nurseries, or friends may offer to give you pieces of root runners. These should be planted in spring using a good potting compost. Place the pot on a window facing south, east or west. Cut off the top few centimetres of the stem for a bushy plant.

culinary

Cook spearmint leaves with potatoes, carrots peas and cauliflower. Apple mint is very good when shredded over salads or mixed into cottage cheese and yoghurt. An excellent mint sauce can be made combining spearmint, apple mint and wine vinegar. Eau de Cologne garnishes cool summer drinks. Add it to sweet omelettes and souffles and fresh fruit salad. All varieties can be rubbed into roast meat joints and poultry.

medicinal

Teas made from all the mints are known to ease indigestion and settle upset tummies. Fresh leaves rubbed on the forehead are said to relieve head-aches. An infusion of spearmint leaves can be used as a lotion to improve the complexion; added to bath water it is supposed to invigorate the bather.

historical

For centuries Arabs have drunk mint tea to stimulate their virility. Gerard says: 'Mint is whole-some for the stomach. It is good for watering eyes. It is poured into the ears with honied water'. In Greek mythology the nymph Menthe was changed into mint by Pluto's jealous wife.

Parsley

Parsley is my favourite herb. The sweet tangy flavour bursts out as you eat it. I could devour a plateful in one go. There are several varieties of parsley. All are biennial and can grow up to 30cm (12"). The plants have bright green foliage and produce small yellow-green flowers in the second year. The curled moss variety (the young plants opposite) has deeply divided, curly leaves, while the fern leaf variety has flat leaves which give a pretty, lacy effect.

cultivation

Read the notes on cultivation (page 2). Germination takes a little longer than usual, but I believe it unnecessary to scald seeds with boiling water. When the seedlings produce their first two leaves they can be transplanted into a parsley pot; put two or three in each hole. Allow the plant some sun for at least part of the day.

culinary

Few dishes aren't improved by the addition of parsley. Four tomatoes stuffed with 3 tablespoons of chopped parsley, a clove of crushed garlic, 2 tablespoons of breadcrumbs and 2 of oil will accompany most fish or meat dishes. Parsley also brings out the flavour of other herbs and will garnish virtually anything, especially rather bland dishes. Parsley sauce is excellent with fresh vegetables, cauliflower, sprouts, and so on, as well as fish.

medicinal

Parsley contains vitamins A, B and C, proteins and iron., Chewing the fresh leaves should dispel the lingering taste of garlic and onions. A tea can be made which is said to ease arthritis and rheumatism. Parsley tablets may be bought from most herbalists as a urinary tonic.

historical

The Romans wore parsley garlands at their feasts to prevent drunkenness. Because parsley is rather slow to germinate, it was believed that the seed went to the devil and back seven times before it appeared above the ground. Where parsley thrives, the woman is boss, or so the saying goes.

Scented Geranium

The two varieties of geranium illustrated opposite are the rose and lemon. The rose has bright green, soft, slightly hairy leaves with deeply cut edges. Small pink flowers bloom in midsummer. The leaves of the lemon are a similar shape but smaller, the centres are lime-green and outer edges cream.

cultivation

I have yet to find a merchant who sells scented geranium seeds. Plants can be bought at nurseries, from which cuttings may be taken — detach a stem, including the heel, and remove the flower leaves. Put this into a coffee cup of moist compost and cover with polythene. When new leaves appear, remove the bag. Repot when the plant outgrows the cup.

culinary

Both these geraniums have a delicate aromatic flavour with a tinge of spice. The washed leaves can be chopped and added to fresh fruit salad, ice cream, plain yoghurt and cream or cottage cheese. The flavour of crab-apple jelly is greatly enhanced by placing a leaf (of either variety) at the bottom of the jar, pouring in the liquid jelly and putting another leaf on top. Seal in the usual way.

medicinal

As far as I know the scented geranium is without medicinal qualities, but as most edible herbs are favoured with health-giving properties, perhaps these are too. They certainly add something special to home-made cool drinks.

historical

The rose geranium is a native of South Africa and came to Europe in the seventeenth century. Both varieties have been used since then as one of the many ingredients for potpourris. By the mid-nineteenth century a rose geranium was being cultivated on a wide scale by the French for their perfume industry.

Summer Savory

sunny position is preferred. Take care not to squash the pot between other herbs or the plant's bushiness will be retarded.

culinary

The leaves of summer savory have a peppery, spicy taste. In the Middle Ages the plant was used for flavouring trout, but it is now thought of as the traditional bean herb. Haricot, runner, French and broad beans are all improved by the addition of savory, which brings out the flavour (particularly if the beans are frozen) and helps digestion. The herb is also used with pork, cucumber salad, thick soups; it makes an excellent herb vinegar.

medicinal

Summer savory contains an oil which aids digestion and is suitable for use with any food which is difficult to digest. You can make a tea from the fresh or dried leaves. This has been recommended as a general tonic or as a gargle for sore throats.

Summer savory is a tender annual which grows wild in the Mediterranean but is rarely found in Britain. It reaches a height of 30cm (12"). Its small narrow leaves are formed sparsely along rigid stems. Tiny mauve or white flowers grow in the axils of the leaves and bloom from July to September.

historical

The Romans introduced the savories (the winter and summer varieties) to Britain. The plants were used in cooking before hot oriental spices were imported. Savory was a popular Saxon culinary herb and was later applied as an external antiseptic.

cultivation

Read the general notes on cultivation (page 2). The seeds should germinate within a week to ten days of sowing. If they are sown in June the plant will be ready to use with home-grown beans. A

Basil

Sweet basil is a half-hardy annual which grows up to 60cm (24"). It originated in South East Asia and has been used as a medicinal and culinary herb in Europe for nearly two thousand years. The leaves are large, shiny, bulging and frequently appear to flop. They are cool and soft to the touch. The spiked flowers are creamy white and bloom from late July to late September. House flies dislike basil and a sprig hung in the wardrobe is supposed to keep moths at bay.

cultivation

Read notes on cultivation (page 2). The seeds should germinate within a week to ten days. The plants will require your sunniest window sill and must be turned on alternate days so that all the foliage receives some warmth and light. It is best to water from the bottom. Pinch out the flowering spikes to encourage bushy growth.

culinary

Pick the leaves from the top of the plant. The flavour (spicy, pungent and sweet) becomes stronger when cooked. Basil is frequently used in Italian dishes. It is especially good with tomatoes — shred some fresh leaves over buttered tomatoes and mushrooms just before grilling. Also add shredded basil and a clove of crushed garlic to salad dressings and spaghetti sauces. Fresh leaves are delicious in wholewheat bread and cheddar cheese sandwiches.

medicinal

An infusion of fresh basil leaves is said to be excellent for indigestion. It is also reputed to quell excessive vomiting and, if taken before a journey, to prevent travel sickness. In the Far East it is used as a remedy for kidney disorders and made into soothing compresses.

historical

The Greek word *basileus* means king and the plant was favoured above all others herbs. A French physician once stated that one of his acquaintances bred a scorpion in his brain simply by smelling basil. In northern France basil is a traditional gift among farmers' wives, and is used to discourage flies.

Sweet Marjoram

Sweet (or knotted) marjoram is a low-growing annual which reaches about 20cm (8"). It has small green leaves and thin woody stems. The flowers are rather odd; like little knots, tiny petals peep from green balls and look as if they were trying desperately to open, but never seem to make it.

cultivation

Read notes on cultivation (page 2). Seeds should germinate within a week to ten days. Ensure that small plants never become too dry, the roots will die quite quickly. Put the plants on a west or east facing windowsill; sun all day will cause the leaves to droop. Marjoram is not a hardy herb but it will survive if a little care is taken.

culinary

Sweet marjoram is milder than oregano (wild marjoram) and has a sweet, slightly peppery flavour. Dry marjoram, frequently sold in groceries, bears little resemblance in flavour to the fresh leaf. Use this herb generously in liver and other strong meat dishes. Casserole cubed pork in cider with garlic and a covering of chopped leaves. Marjoram blends well with thyme for stuffings and sauces and is delicious with cucumber salad.

medicinal

Marjoram contains a volatile oil which is said to act as a mild tonic. A tea made from the fresh leaves is said to relieve nervous headaches and encourage perspiration in feverish colds and flu. The dried leaves are sometimes powdered and taken as snuff to clear nasal congestion.

historical

In a Greek myth, Armarkos dropped a jar of perfume and was changed into marjoram by the gods. Venus pitied him and when she touched the plant it produced the delicate flavour and scent we know today. For centuries the herb has been used as a preserver. Marjoram means 'joy of the mountains.'

Borage

Borage, a native of southern Europe, is a hardy annual and grows to between 30 and 75 cm (12" — 30"). It is sometimes found growing wild on waste land. The grey-green leaves are large, oval and covered with stiff white hairs, as are the hollow stems. The pretty star-shaped flowers are usually brilliant blue, but it is not uncommon to find a bright pink or white one flowering on the same plant. They bloom profusely from July to November and often later if the winter is mild.

cultivation

Read notes on cultivation (page 2). Borage seeds germinate very quickly; inspect the cups morning and night or the seedlings may become straggly and must then be discarded. The plant will seed its self and the little seedlings which spring up in the plant pot may be transplanted for the following year.

culinary

The young leaves have a slight flavour of cucumber. They can be chopped finely and added to salads or cottage cheese. You can cook them as a vegetable, eat them on their own or add them to cabbage and spinach. Try dipping whole leaves into batter and frying them to give borage fritters. The flowers are also edible and can be sprinkled over salads, candied to make delicate sweets and cake decorations or added to cool home-made summer drinks.

medicinal

An infusion can be made from fresh borage leaves. Sweeten it with a little clear honey and a freshly squeezed lemon or orange. This tea is said to increase the flow of milk in nursing mothers and be beneficial to the digestive system. It is also supposed to prevent catarrh.

historical

As long ago as Roman times, borage was alleged to relieve and cure the mind and the body. John Gerard (1545-1612), the English herbalist, wrote: 'The leaves and flowers put into wine make men and women glad and merry, driving away all sadness, dulness and melancholy.'

First published in Great Britain in 1978
Search Press Limited, Wellwood, North Farm Road,
Tunbridge Wells, Kent TN2 3DR

Text and drawings by Polly Pinder

Reprinted 1987

**New edition, slightly revised, reprinted
in larger format 1989**

Reprinted 1990, 1993

ISBN 0 85532 668 9

Printed in Spain by A. G. Elkar, S. Coop, 48012 Bilbao